SH!T
YOU NEED
TO KNOW
THAT NOBODY
BOTHERED
TO TELL YOU

T0015554

SH!T

YOU NEED TO KNOW THAT NOBODY BOTHERED TO TELL YOU

A Perpetual Guide to Life for Everyone

CLARK MERRILL

MEDIA

MEDIA

Published 2022 by Gildan Media LLC
aka G&D Media
www.GandDmedia.com

FIRST EDITION 2022

Front cover design by David Rheinhardt of Pyrographx

Interior design by Meghan Day Healey of Story Horse, LLC

Library of Congress Cataloging-in-Publication Data is available upon request

ISBN: 978-1-7225-0592-9

10   9   8   7   6   5   4   3   2   1

*This book was written for my niece
Katelyn Rose and all her friends.*

*It was inspired by my wife Colleen;
I miss her every second of every day
since she left us.*

Contents

Part Two

In-Laws, Neighbors, and
General Relationship Advice

❧

Part Three

Money, Career, and General Life Advice

Introduction

I grew up in the seventies. The midpoint for us baby boomers.

Suffice to say that our parents didn't have much of a choice about having kids. The formula was: have sex, have kids. There wasn't much they could do about it. So they had kids, and we didn't come with instructions. It was a learn as you go process for most of them, my parents included. They learned from each other. There was no Internet, no place of stored knowledge, and quite often they messed up. When they did, we, the kids, saw this as our "normal." We all lamented about what our parents had done to us, and the statement "*When I grow up and have kids . . .*" was our way of coping and prepping for our turn at bat.

But certain things happened in the sixties and seventies: the Pill, *Roe v. Wade*, entire rows in drug and convenience stores devoted to condoms and birth control. You didn't have to go to your druggist and give the secret word for a condom (*raincoat* was the secret word at our local drugstore) and pray that he didn't tell your parents. It was a radical shift.

Yes, the myth is true. We were the generation of sex, drugs, and rock and roll. It was great for about ten years. Then the pendulum swung back the other way with HIV/AIDS, herpes, and a whole litany of incurable sex-related diseases. The party was over! But we now had choices about having kids, and many of us chose not to, or at least to put it off for a while.

That was good and bad. We had time to experience more of life, but we basically still had the child-rearing knowledge of our parents. Now don't get me wrong: not everything our parents did was bad or wrong; some were exceptional at raising kids. A lot weren't, but they did their best they could with what they had. I think back on my childhood. I can identify missed opportunities, gaps of knowledge and common sense that, if I had had access to them, might have saved me tons of grief and time.

This does not mean that my parents were bad people or that I had a terrible childhood. Not at all. My parents were good people, who did the best they could, and my childhood was the best it could be under those circumstances. I learned the hard way.

The hard way is not necessarily a bad way to learn. But if it is the only way to learn life's big and little lessons, it can be extremely frustrating.

For these reasons, when I was about ten years old, I started looking for a book that had all of life's answers: answers to all the things that were happening to and around me, like the deaths of friends and relatives, the sudden importance of the opposite sex (to this day I still have a hard time talking to them), getting married.

I asked about such a book in the library and was handed works by Emily Post, Ann Landers, and Dale Carnegie—all fine books, but none with the answers I was seeking, and honestly, just a little above my fifth-grade reading level.

I never did find my book with the answers.

As I got older, I sought out mentors in life. I found two: Dick Finely (I dated his daughter for a short—very short—time) and David Samee, my first real boss and friend. Both were older than me and had the patience to listen to my queries and answer without judgment. They were my life mentors until they died. I miss them both very much.

From age ten to now, I have learned a lot of the answers I was seeking (certainly not all: I am still learning and getting knocked around). And I realized that it was time to pay it forward. Maybe keeping someone from having to learn everything the hard way, as I did.

Enter my niece Katelyn.

I've known Katelyn all of her life. My wife, Colleen, was her godmother (Katelyn called her "my fairy godmother"). They were very close. Katelyn and I, not so much. The extent of our conversations occurred during Easter, Thanksgiving, and Christmas. They were: "Merry Christmas, Katelyn"; "Merry Christmas, Clark" (no "uncle" was my choice, as I thought that that word would create a sense of obligation with no real personal relationship).

That relationship existed until she was thirteen. When she reached that age, her mother, Kathy (my wife's sister), came to me and said, "Clark, I want you to tutor Katelyn in science."

I said, "No, I train adults. I don't know anything about science, and I don't really like kids."

She reminded me that the year before she had saved my life: she was a nurse, and my wife called her to stabilize me and call the ambulance when I was hit with an unknown staph infection that went septic and left me convulsing. She asked me again. I, of course, said, "OK." What else could I say?

Katelyn arrived at my house the next week. I walked in to find her sitting on her hands at the kitchen table, staring down at her science books. I said hello; she said hi.

"Why are you here?" I asked.

"Because my mother made me come."

"That makes two of us, but why are you *really* here?"

"Because I am failing science."

"Who cares! You don't want to be a scientist, do you? Just fail and move on to something you like."

"I can't. If I fail science, I have to repeat the eighth grade."

"So what? Just repeat the eighth grade. You'll be even better at everything!"

"I can't. I won't be able to go to high school with my friends."

"So you are really here to pass science so that you can graduate from the eighth grade and go to high school with your friends?"

"Yes."

"OK, so what is your grade in science?"

"F."

"What do we need to pass?"

She looked at me sheepishly. "An A?"

I shook my head. "We will never go from a F to an A."

She tried again. "A B?"

"Forget it."

She was getting frustrated. "A C?"

"Nope."

Finally, she asked, "A D?"

I nodded. "If you got a D-minus, would you pass science and be able to go to high school with your friends?"

"Yes."

"OK. We can go from a F to a D-minus, no problem. You pass science, and you get to go to high school with your friends.

But you have to promise to *never, ever* get an A or B on any science test or quiz!"

That confused her, and she furrowed her brow. "Why?"

"If you do, your mother will raise the bar. We don't need that. We just need the D-minus. You pass science and go to high school with your friends, and your mother is happy!"

"OK!" She smiled.

I had never seen a thirteen-year-old get excited before, but she did. I promised her that we would not waste time on anything that might be useless in her life plans and that I would give her questions to ask that would be fun for her and embarrassing to her teacher.

So what happened? Katelyn did get a B on a quiz, and we had a heart-to-heart about that (after her mother came jumping into the house, screaming, "Katelyn got a B, Katelyn got a B!").

By the end of the eighth grade, Katelyn made the honor roll, got the award for the most improved student at the annual assembly, and became the de facto spokesperson for her science class by continually challenging the science text and her teacher. She went to high school with her friends, got accepted to three colleges, and has just received her BS in business from Massachusetts' Salem State University (I don't think her parents were planning on her taking the college path).

Katelyn and I became very close because I listened to her, talked to her, and related to her frustrations about life. That is how I got to know her, and that is why we still talk a lot. She knows that I will listen, not judge, and offer advice only when she asks. (She asks a lot.)

She asked me to write this book for her and her friends. So here goes, with no promises other than the stories that I tell are absolutely true and not based on a regurgitated story from someone else or *Mushroom Soup for Your Soul*.

Katelyn and I hope you and your friends will find something useful in this book.

Part One

✳

Dating, Weddings, Funerals, and Other Annoying Life Events

✳

1

Dating

You are who you are.
They are who they are. Period!

When I was young, there was Miss Right and Miss Right Now. Getting them confused caused me problems. Nobody ever explained the difference. Especially the drastic effects that hormones can have on judgment and decision making. (Cue in Meat Loaf's "Paradise by the Dashboard Light.")

I was standing at the altar, watching her walk down the aisle.

John, my brother and best man, whispered in my ear, "Bro, let's go now. Just hop in my car, and we can explain everything later."

I didn't respond. I should have.

I knew he was right. Although my fiancée and I had known each other for three and a half years and lived together for one and a half years, deep down I knew I was getting married mostly out of a sense of obligation. Sure, we could fix each other and maybe, eventually, fall deeply in love and live happily ever after, just like in all the books and movies.

Bad idea. She was, and still is, a good person. But standing there at the altar, I knew that she wasn't the one for me. John knew it, and maybe deep down, she knew it.

We stayed together for seven years, trying to make it right. Eventually I had to admit that my brother was right, and the best thing to do was split up. It was the hardest decision of my young life and was challenging and unfair to her.

Where did it go off the rails?

At dating.

Let's talk about when you're dating. The first rule is: *people rarely change, and then only with great trauma or extreme effort.*

You are what you are, and to plan a long-term relationship with the idea that "I'm going to change that person or myself" is a really bad idea.

They may wish to change, but very rarely do. We are who we are. That was set in our psyche growing up. By the time we're eight or nine, we pretty much have our values and how we make our decisions. Changing that, no matter how much we may want to, is next to impossible.

If you're looking at someone as having "potential," it's not going to happen. It'll just lead to heartbreak. If you're going to have a relationship with someone, love them the way they are, not the way you want them to be.

Remember:

You are who you are.
They are who they are. Period!

2

Meeting the Future In-Laws

*Offer to pay, but be gracious
when they insist, and let them pay.*

Colleen was twenty-one.

I was thirty-two.

Colleen was a Catholic who had never been married.

I was a divorced Protestant.

Colleen was a restaurant manager.

I was an executive for the same restaurant chain.

She lived at home with her parents.

I had my own apartment two miles away.

Chances of a successful relationship: .0002 percent.

I knew she was Miss Right for me. (I was sure to take my time after my first attempt ended with a divorce.)

After six months of dating, we decided that I should meet her mother. I chose to do it alone, in case it went horribly wrong.

I walked up the steps onto the porch, rang the bell, and hoped lightning would strike me dead before her mother answered.

It didn't.

She opened the door and I said, "Hi. I'm Clark."

With a somber face, she said, "Like Kent?"

"No. Like Gable!"

She smiled. (I knew she loved *Gone with the Wind* and Clark Gable).

I will tell you that it wasn't all roses from then on, but at least Colleen and I had a chance. And later on, her mother was my sponsor when I converted to Catholicism.

During that meeting I suggested that we go to dinner. We made plans. Colleen and I and my future in-laws, went; my mother was in town for a visit, so that made five.

It was all good until . . .

Who pays? You pay? I pay?

Offer to pay, but be gracious when they insist, and let them pay.

There will come a time in the relationship where, God willing, the future in-laws will be around, and you're going to meet them. You'll probably go out to dinner—and this is for the guys, OK? When you go out to dinner, the guy thing is you want to pay (it's testosterone). You're going to say, "I'll pick up the check."

Don't. Don't pick up the check!

Offer to pick it up, and be prepared to pay if they say yes (leave a really good tip, because they'll look at it over your shoulder). But in all likelihood the father or mother of your future bride will say, "I've got it."

Do not argue with them.

Graciously say, "Thank you. I really appreciate it." And let them pay. Don't duke it out. (That's really bad, because they'll see the future with you is nothing but an argument.)

This is their way of showing their son or daughter that they want to contribute to the rest of your lives together. They still want to take care of things.

So the key to going out to dinner and meeting the parents for the first time, or even the second time, is to offer to pay; be prepared to pay. But if they want to pay, let them, be gracious, and thank them graciously.

You are setting the scene for interacting in the future. It's not just one night and it's not about who has the most testosterone to win the battle. That's a losing scenario. So let them pay.

Offer to pay, but be gracious
when they insist, and let them pay.

3

The Wedding Plan

Every wedding needs a mission statement.

My future mother-in-law and I were working on the seating chart for the wedding reception.

For some unexplainable reason (maybe because my friends and family were flying up from Miami to Boston), it was important to me who was sitting at what table.

I was from Miami. All of Colleen's friends and family were from New England. It was a Catholic wedding, and most of my friends were Protestant or Jewish.

The seating chart discussion quickly got heated.

Colleen came in from the other room. She wasn't happy. She reminded me that we had written a mission statement for our wedding right after we were engaged and we had given it to everybody.

She pulled out her copy and handed it to me.

It read: "To have a joyous day!"

"Is this adding to having a joyous event?" she asked.

I said, "No." I turned to her mother and said, "Please, just seat them wherever you believe is best, so they will share in our joyous day."

Her mother looked up and smiled. Crisis averted.

We used our mission statement a number of times in making decisions: the band, the food, the caterer—everything.

The manager was telling us that we only needed two valet parkers, but we wanted more. I knew that there would be a lot of people driving and arriving at once. We didn't want them sitting there, waiting in their cars for the valet, or waiting for the valet to retrieve their cars at the end of the night. We wanted more valets, and we were willing to pay to make sure that our guests got in and out quickly, which made it a joyous event. The manager understood. Mission accomplished.

Weddings are stressful. No matter what, there's going to be stress. When you get two families involved and a bunch of people making decisions, it's going to be stressful.

The first thing is to write a mission statement for the event with your partner. This may sound overly businesslike or even silly. But when my Colleen and

I got married, we sat down and wrote the mission statement: "To have a joyous day."

Our focus became clear. Every decision we made was based on the question, "Does this add to it being a joyous day?" And we and our guests did have a very joyous day!

Every wedding needs a mission statement.

4

The Wedding

It's about the guests, stupid!

Most of us are brought up to see weddings as the bride's day. That is a bad idea—absolutely the wrong focus.

Now this may be a bit controversial, but I learned early on that if a wedding is about the bride, usually it is pretty miserable. There's a lot of drama, and certainly the bride is beautiful, but for a guest, it's boring. Sometimes I just eat and leave.

The wedding is about the guests. Period. They're there to support you for the rest of your life and acknowledge that this marriage is a really great commitment for the two of you.

So make it about the guests. Everything is about your guests. How can we make it fun for them? How can we keep them engaged? How can we keep them from not waiting for hour after hour for the photographer to finish taking pictures, or for the videographer to do whatever they're doing? How do we make sure that the guests are having fun and remember our wedding as a terrific event?

Colleen and I were both in the restaurant and ice cream business. She ran a very successful ice cream restaurant, and I sold the franchises for them.

When we were planning our wedding, we talked about the weddings that we'd attended, mostly those of our relatives. We both came from the food service industry. We knew the wedding had to be about the guests. Many came to our wedding from out of town and had no idea what we did or how we met. With that in mind, instead of an open bar, we had an open ice cream sundae bar, where guests could have their own sundaes made by a professional soda jerk.

It was a tremendous success. The facility manager of the country club came to us during the event and said, "I have to figure out how to do this for all of our events! This is great. People love it!" They did!

Weddings must be fun for the guests. We told the photographer that they had forty-five minutes to take all the pictures, and that was it. The photographer started to argue. We said, "Look, we'll get another photographer. You've got forty-five minutes."

After forty-five minutes, I looked at my watch and said, "We're done."

We didn't want to keep our guests waiting. We made sure that everything that we did was fun. To this day, people who came still say it was the best wedding they ever attended.

If you create your wedding so it's about the guests, people will remember it, and that's really what you want them to do: remember that you were married and they had a great time, and they'll be there to support you for the rest of your married lives.

It's about the guests, stupid!

5

Wedding Gifts

Show me the money!

Let's talk about wedding gifts. What gift do you give the bride and groom? Do you give a gift if you don't show up? Well, the answer to that is yes. You give a gift. Even if you don't go to the wedding.

What's an appropriate gift?

Most couples have a bridal registry at different stores and websites. They will tell you or send out a list.

You can do that. I have a full service for ten of Noritake Rothschild porcelain dinner service, with everything you need to host a banquet. Now don't get me wrong: it's beautiful. We've used it exactly once in thirty years, to host another couple for dinner.

In short, the most practical gift is cash.

Give cash or some form of money that they can spend on what they want. It's the most appreciated gift, because all newlyweds have expenses. Gift cards, although more secure, are a pain in the ass to use and can get lost. Give cash or a check. Something that can be put safely away. (Dick, my best friend and mentor, gave us a $500 savings bond. I don't know if you can still get them, but it was great: we had to keep it until it matured. Whatever you do, don't take any investment advice from me or this book. I just thought it was a great gift.)

What's the appropriate amount? A way to figure out the minimum is to estimate the cost for a single dinner serving at the reception and multiply it by the number of guests you are bringing—usually yourself and one other (if invited!). That is the minimum I start with.

It changes from place to place, but right now, where I live, the appropriate wedding gift for a couple is a minimum of $200 to $300. When I go, I give more, because I know that these are young people starting out, and they need all the help they can get. So the appropriate gift is to give cash. If you want to give a little something else too, that's fine. But also give cash.

Where do you put the card?

Look for the gift table at the reception. There's usually a box for the cards, and that's where you put the card with your gift inside. Don't walk around reception with it, looking like, "What am I supposed to do with this right now?" Just put it in the box, and go have fun at the wedding.

Show me the money!

6

The Toast

It's a toast, not a roast.

It was a mid-July evening in New England. I was outside celebrating the recent wedding of good friends. They had a small private wedding and a dinner about a month earlier, which I'd attended. But this was the official reception for everyone. It was hot. I mean temperature wise. There were lots of fans.

The maid of honor stood and delivered a heartfelt, funny, targeted, and short toast to the newlyweds. We laughed, smiled, and drank the toast. She delivered it just the way we talked about it when she was preparing. A home run!

The best man, not to be outdone, stood up, and let loose a droning, forty-five-minute list of inside jokes and boring stories (definitely not funny and totally inappropriate for the crowd). Then he invited the groomsmen up to add their stupid, unrehearsed stories, which, even if they were sober, wouldn't have made any sense to the audience. People started walking away after thirty minutes of this.

They finally finished. I sighed in relief.

The maid of honor, the bride's sister, came over, and I congratulated her on a fantastic toast. She saw, as did the entire audience, the stark contrast between good and bad wedding toasts.

I said, "Watch this. The best man and all the groomsmen are heading to the bar. They are going to high-five and congratulate each other and boast about what a great toast they just made."

Sure enough, that is exactly what happened, as everyone watching rolled their eyes.

Let's say you're going to give a wedding toast, either as the father of the bride, the best man, or the maid of honor. Unless you're a stand-up comic by profession, and people are paying you lots of money to come see your show, don't try to be funny. It's a toast, not a roast. Speak from the heart. Share a short story of why this person and couple are so special to you. Wish them a long, extended, healthy relationship, make the toast, clink the glasses, and sit down.

It's a toast, not a roast.

7

Thanksgiving Tar Pit

It's not just gravy.

I love Thanksgiving. I love the food, the memories, my mom's pumpkin pie—I love it all. But whenever I go to someone's house for Thanksgiving, there's usually some drama going on, and it's usually centered in the kitchen. It may not be a major drama, but you can feel the tension.

One year Colleen and I decided to cook Thanksgiving dinner for our families and friends: about twenty to twenty-three people. Colleen runs a restaurant, and I had twenty one years experience in food service myself, so we know how to prepare a dinner for a large group. We know how to entertain. We throw excellent parties.

I was doing all the cooking. That was the deal, and I'm a pretty good cook. Although I'm not a great cook, I'm a lot better than most, and I do know how to make sure everything comes out hot and at the same time.

All we needed was the gravy. As you know, gravy is one of the most important things for any Thanksgiving dinner. Everything else was hot and going to the table.

I didn't know how to make gravy, I never had to. My mom always made the gravy, and she wasn't here. I went over to Colleen's mother. "Can you come over and show me how to make the gravy?"

"Oh yes, of course I can," she said. She was excited and dying to contribute.

Now here's the thing: every family has their own gravy recipe, and none are the same.

She started. We needed the pan drippings. I got the pan drippings.

Then I said, "We're going to put giblets in it, right?"

She said, "No! No giblets."

Automatically that was a big problem, because *my* mom always put the giblets in the gravy, and I had cooked them for that reason.

Then she said, "We need the water from the green beans."

Another problem. I said, "I threw that out."

She told me she couldn't make it without green-bean water.

This was not going well.

Now I was starting to get upset. We were making gravy without giblets, and now we needed green-bean water that I didn't have.

That's when I realized what the drama is on Thanksgiving—people!

I paused. People need to feel that they are contributing something special and that their recipe is the best.

I was ready to jump in and tell her that *real* Thanksgiving gravy had giblets in it! Instead I decided to smile, keep my mouth shut, and see if I could drain enough water from the green beans we'd already cooked to make the gravy. I did.

I watched intently as she added a little water and flour and poured it into the pot with the drippings (no giblets). She was very specific about her directions with the spoon and flour and water.

We ended up with a quart or a quart and a half of excellent gravy. More importantly, the gravy was her recipe, and it came out the way she wanted. For that meal, my mother-in-law and the gravy were critical contributors.

It's not just true at Thanksgiving. It's true in life. People need to feel important, that what they do matters, and that they are critical contributors in life.

Tell people when we see them doing something well. Let them know that what they're doing is important and that it has positive effects on people and relationships.

It's not just gravy.

8

How to Slice a Turkey

*It's already dead. You don't
need to go Cro-Magnon on it.*

You're invited over to your future in-laws' house, and it's Thanksgiving. They look at you and say, "Would you like the honor of slicing the turkey?"

"Of course!" you say, trying to hide the panic.

Now this is a tough situation, because I can tell you that ninety-nine out of 100 people do not have a clue about properly slicing a turkey. It always ends up looking like some kind of massacre.

People will get their turkey meat, but it's usually not a pretty situation. I've even seen situations where they took the turkey in the kitchen, ripped it apart with their hands, and brought it back out to the table. It was a little Cro-Magnon, if you ask me.

There is a way to slice a turkey. First say, "Thank you," and agree to slice it. Walk up to the turkey, and have a sharp carving knife, a big, long fork, and an empty platter for the meat.

First, slice off the drumstick. Here's a fact: the only people on the planet that like drumsticks are kids and people at medieval fairs. Or if you've had too many beers and say, "I'm going to have a turkey leg and show my manhood." Other than that, nobody eats turkey drumsticks. They're a pain in the ass, and there's really not that much meat on them. (Lots of extra cartilage, which gets in the way.)

So now how do you cut the drumstick off the bird? (You should know that just about everybody calls the Thanksgiving turkey on the table "the bird.") First, pull it back and away from the breast, and you'll hear a little crack. It'll expose the knuckle: the joint. Take the knife, and slice through the joint. It's all cartilage. Then you slice around the leg, and it will come off. Set that at the top of the platter.

There are two kinds of meat in a turkey: white meat and dark meat. Everyone says they love white meat. The white meat comes from the turkey's breast. For me, turkey white meat sucks. It's usually dry, because whoever cooked the turkey really didn't have a clue about what they're doing. They didn't baste it properly and relied much too heavily on the name "Butterball" to do all of the work. Sometimes it's moist, and it can be OK. But it's usually the first part of the bird to dry out.

I like dark meat. Where does the dark meat come from? It comes from the thigh of the turkey. That's what the drumstick was attached to.

Let's do the white meat first. Bring your knife parallel to the table. (Not perpendicular. Perpendicular is if you're going to stab the bird. We are slicing it). Bring the knife down the side of the turkey's breast to where the knuckle of the drumstick was. Then you just cut a slice in, depending on the size of the bird, anywhere from two to three and a half inches, maybe four. Nothing comes off yet.

Go up to the top of the breast, right on the outside. Now we're slicing downward, about a quarter of an inch thick. Slice down to the inward slice that you just made. The slice will fall onto your fork. Using your fork and knife, set the slice on a platter next to the drumstick. Do that for the entire turkey breast on one side. Don't do the whole turkey. We're just carving the one side.

Now it's time to get the dark meat. The dark meat is on the thighs. (The thigh starts where you cut off the drumstick and attaches to just below the breast on the bottom of the bird.)

Take the fork, and pull the thighbone out a little bit. Then start slicing downward. Make the slices about a quarter an inch thick. It will be messier than the white meat, but hang in there. Everyone will be so impressed with your drumstick and white meat display that they won't notice any dark meat imperfections. Now place the dark meat slices separately from the white meat on the platter. You might need to pull the bone out a little bit to get on the inside, and eventually you can cut it off.

The last thing on that side of the turkey is the wing. The way we cut the wing is the same way we cut the drumstick. You might want to use your hands to pull the wing opposite of where it's folded. Again, it will expose the knuckle, and you cut where the knuckle is. Place the wing next to the drumstick on the platter.

Now picture the platter: We have a drumstick on the upper left part. We put the wing on the upper right part. Down the center, we have the white breast meat, and then the dark meat. And that's half of the turkey. That's how to slice the turkey and look like a pro!

It's already dead. You don't need to go Cro-Magnon on it.

9

Pumpkin Pie

You just have to ask. Sometimes the secret is in plain sight!

I love my mom's pumpkin pie. My mom made the best pumpkin pie in the world. At Thanksgiving, between Thursday and Saturday my brother and I ate fifteen whole pumpkin pies. That's how much we loved this pie. We'd eat it like pizza. It was the best ever.

When Colleen and I got together, I told the story of my mom's great pumpkin pie for Thanksgiving and how nobody could ever match it. No store-bought pie, no restaurant pie, not anyone ever made a pumpkin pie that was anywhere close to as good as my mom's.

A couple of years after we were married, Colleen decided she would make me a pumpkin pie just like my mom's. She made this pie. I tried it, and it was really good, but not the same as my mom's.

The next year she tried again, looking through cookbooks and asking people for the best recipes. Again, it wasn't the same. She did this for about six years, and they were all good pies, but they weren't my mom's pie. I couldn't eat fifteen of them.

Finally, she said she wanted to call my mom and ask her for this recipe, but she thought it was a family secret. I said, "Give it a shot. Maybe she will tell you." They were pretty close.

A couple of days later, she handed me a slice of pumpkin pie. I ate it. It was as if I was fifteen again. Honest to God. It was just amazing.

"Oh my God, this is my mom's pie. You know, I'm just like a little kid. How many did you make?" I asked, thinking I would eat twelve. I know, I was way too old to be eating twelve pumpkin pies, but I could have done it.

"Did my mom give you the secret?"

"Oh, yeah. She gave me the secret."

"What was it?"

"The secret is to go to the grocery store and buy a can of Libby's pumpkin. And on the side of the can is a recipe. Do everything the recipe says. That's how to make the pie."

I started laughing. "You mean I could have made this?"

Colleen was happy; I was happy.

The reality is that all we have to do is ask. The worst that can happen is that they can say no. But we have to ask.

The other side of the coin is that sometimes the secret's printed on the side of the can. We've just got to look at the side of the can and have faith that it's good.

You just have to ask. Sometimes the secret is in plain sight!

10

Six Steps to Restaurant Wine: The Basics

Follow the steps, and don't show off!

Ordering wine in a restaurant can be an intimidating experience if you are clueless. It can make even the most confident person self-conscious.

Here is a step-by-step guide I use to get through the experience.

First, if you are a wine expert, back off a little bit. You're not there to impress everyone with how much you know about wine. Just order the wine!

Most of us aren't experts.

Usually the person who orders the wine is the one who is expecting (or expected) to pick up the tab. If you're ordering wine for the whole table, here are the steps to follow:

The first thing to decide is what kind of wine you're going to order: red or white.

Red wines are meant for red meat or hearty dishes, and white wines are for poultry and fish. Rosés are for nobody. Well, not for a whole table, anyway. (Friends don't let friends drink rosé.)

Red wine is served at room temperature, and white wine is chilled. Never have a red wine chilled. And if a white wine comes out warm, you might want to send it back to get a chilled bottle.

Now that you've decided the color of wine you're ordering for the table, the sommelier or your waiter will hand you a wine list. (The sommelier is the wine steward, most common in extremely expensive restaurants.) This book can be a hundred pages in some restaurants. Most are two to four pages. Don't get intimidated.

Let's say you're ordering red wines. Find the section called "Red Wine." So far, so good. It's usually divided into the types of grape, and that has to do with how strong the taste is. Don't worry: picking "red" is a good enough start.

Within each category, the wines are listed by price. That's the second choice to make: how much you want to spend on a bottle of wine. If you're picking up the check, you know what your price range is. If someone else is paying, get an idea of what everyone is going to order for dinner to help guide your selection and price range.

Never go for either the cheapest or the most expensive wine. You usually want to be in the top third of the price range. If everyone is on a really tight budget, it's OK to go lower, but don't get the cheapest one.

Also, don't get sticker shock from the prices. They're going to be twice what you pay in a retail wine shop. You're paying for the wine and the service—someone to bring it to you and serve it to you and your guests.

Now that you have the color of wine and your price range, ask the sommelier or wait-person what they would recommend based on what most people are ordering for dinner. Then, as he or she is recommending, look for ones that fall in your price range.

Sommeliers are professional wine experts; they aren't just there to sell you the most expensive wine. Look at what they recommend and then choose one that's in your price range.

I do this. Even if my favorite wine is on the menu. Why? Because it gives me a chance to try a new wine. Also if the wine sucks, you know, I didn't pick it.

Now you've ordered the wine, and they bring it to the table. Let the show begin!

They present you the bottle to show you that it's what you ordered and it's not open. If it's not what you ordered, politely tell them. They might say it's a substitute and explain why. You can go with their substitution or not; I usually do. Your choice. In any case, you have to remember what you ordered.

The waiter then uncorks the wine. The top has a lead cap. They cut off the lead. Then, using a corkscrew, they remove the cork. Now they'll set the bottle down, unscrew the cork from the corkscrew, and hand it to you.

You're probably thinking, "What am I going to do with a cork? Why is there even a cork in the first place?"

When the wine is stored, they lay it down on its side. This is so that the wine can circulate through the cork, adding to its distinct flavor.

Hold the cork and smell it. It will be a preview of what the wine tastes like. If it smells like vinegar, there's something wrong with the wine. You hand the cork back and politely say, "I think there might be something wrong here. Would you take a look?" They'll smell it. If they agree there's something wrong with it, they'll take the bottle back and bring you another one.

If it smells OK, you squeeze the cork. You want it to be moist at the end and not dried out. This tells you that it was stored properly. If the cork is dry, it means the wine was stored standing up. (Not usually a major problem, but good to know.) Set the cork down.

Usually I set mine down next to my glass. The next thing they'll do is pour a little bit of the wine in your glass for you to taste before serving the rest of the table. This is to make sure that the wine is not spoiled.

Don't gulp it down, but swirl it in the glass first. It releases the bouquet (that's the smell of the wine). Hold the glass up, and take a deep sniff through your nose. You're smelling the bouquet. If it smells like vinegar, do not taste! Hand it to the sommelier quietly and ask their opinion.

Next swirl the wine again, and hold it up to the light (say the candle on the table). You're looking for how the wine falls on the inside of the glass. That will tell you about its body of the wine. If it just slides right down, it's a light-bodied wine. If it's slow-moving and makes streaks inside the glass—what I call cathedrals, with peaks and valleys—it's a full-bodied wine. (Nobody at the table really cares, but it looks pretty impressive when you do it.)

Now take a sip. Do not gulp; just take a sip. If you swirl it in your mouth a little, that will release more bouquet, and you'll get another smelling sensation (too much to explain now; just trust me on this). Does it taste OK? Or does it taste like vinegar? Is there a problem here?

Assuming that it's all right, we'll say. "Very good." Then they will pour the wine, usually starting with women first. You will be the last.

They will set the bottle next to you. If you finish your glass before everyone else, because you happen to really love that wine and did a great job, do not pour yourself more wine. Wait for the waiter to come and pour the remaining wine, usually around the table, with you being last.

If everyone likes the wine, you did a good job, and you may want to order another bottle (if you are picking up the check!). I prefer to stick with the same one. Don't jump off the cliff here.

If you do this, your friends will see you as the wine expert of the group. Have a great time.

Six steps:

1. Red or white.
2. Price range.
3. Sommelier/waiter suggestions.
4. Select; remember your choice.
5. Cork: wet or dry; vinegar smell?
6. Swirl, smell, taste, serve.

Follow the steps, and don't show off!

11

Wakes

Be there for your friends first!

There are some certainties in all of our lives: You will fall in love. They will break your heart. Your friends will get engaged, get married, have kids, have christenings, a bris, and first birthdays. The kids will graduate high school and college, get married, and so on. We will discuss the things you should know about each. But let's start with the toughest situation you can face in the beginning of adulthood: wakes and funerals.

In the fall of 1976, I was twenty-one years old. I drove to the house of my friends Greg and Carolyn for a visit. Carolyn came running out, shouting that I had to get over to Ron and Val's house right away. Carolyn was Ron and Val's niece.

"Why?"

"Little Ronnie died. Now go!"

Ron and Val were close friends; I'd spent every Friday and Saturday night with them since I was fourteen. I babysat for their kids, Cindy and Ronnie, since they were seven and eight years old. I was really close to "Little" Ronnie, who was a teenager now. He was popular, good-looking, and funny, a bit of a smart-ass, with a great wit.

That three-minute, half-mile drive seemed to take hours. In that short drive, I remembered every conversation Little Ronnie and I had had. Now he was gone. It couldn't be true.

I pulled up to their house and knew it was true from all the expressions on people's faces in the front yard. Expressions I had never seen before. I was in for—and unprepared for—a new and shitty life experience.

Little Ronnie died in a hunting accident in the Everglades. It was his dream to go hunting with his dad. This was his dream come true.

At the hunting camp, he was sitting on the hood of a car, listening to late afternoon hunting stories. As he slid off the car, the breach of his one-barrel shotgun hit the bumper and went off. He was bent over the top of the gun.

He didn't have a chance. They radioed for emergency services. They came as quickly as they could, but he was in the middle of the Everglades. Nobody's fault. It was as true an accident as there ever was.

None of this helped. I didn't know what to say or do; I was in shock.

At the wake and funeral, I was useless as a close family friend. I didn't know what to do. I didn't know how to act. There was no one to ask, and no one stepped up (for good reason: they were dealing with their own shock and grief). There was no book of instructions on how to act or what to expect.

I miss Little Ron to this day and find myself wondering what kind of great life he would have had given the chance.

This is what I learned about wakes. These are occasions when loved ones and friends gather, usually in the presence of the casket of the deceased. They generally take place in funeral homes.

Wakes are important. Make yourself go! It's important to you and especially to the friends and family of the deceased. They will remember.

Upon arrival, sign the guest book if there is one.

Look for the line attending on the deceased. Go to the back of the line. Do not cut the line.

While in line, look around. Don't initiate conversation, but politely answer any questions from anyone around you.

When you get to the head of the line, there is usually a casket. It will be open or closed. Do not comment (or mumble under your breath) about either. You can either kneel or stand: your choice. Either way, face the casket, bow your head, and say a prayer (or look like you are). Show respect at all times.

When you get to the head of the line, you will usually find the most important relatives: mother, father, husband, wife. You have twelve seconds or less—that's it—to speak. Most people freeze and then babble on incoherently about everything they know about the deceased, making the wait time in line even longer.

Here's an outline of what to say:

"I am (name). I am truly sorry for your loss. I knew/worked with (deceased) at (where or how you knew them). (One brief positive incident, story, or memory about the deceased.) Again, I am so sorry for your loss."

This is *not* the place to have a conversation. It is a place to show respect and connection to the family.

There may be a long line of relatives. You don't need to tell each of them the story (they probably don't care and are grieving themselves); just keep moving. Grasp their hand and say, "I am truly sorry for your loss."

I have two or three stories just in case some else down the line asks how I knew the deceased. I have the additional stories so that I don't sound like a recording.

Who speaks if you are a couple, or you are with someone?

The person that was personally closest to the deceased speaks for the couple. They introduce themselves and their partner. Often we are overwhelmed with grief and have a true desire to help. If we are not careful, we can make offers of help that can be received as insincere, even though they are not meant that way.

Here is what *not* to say:

"If there is anything I can do, just let me know."

This sounds good, but if you are truly their friend, they already know this. If you are not a good friend, just a good acquaintance, then it comes off as clichéd and insincere. Your actions will speak for you. If you really mean it, do something for them. Don't make them ask.

What to say or do if you are representing the family at the head of the receiving line?

You might be thinking, "I'm young, and the chances that I am at the head of the line are slim." True. But you might get moved to the head of the line if the people or person ahead of you have to leave (for a bio break or to sit down and compose themselves). In that situation, what do you do?

Relax. Here is what to do: Greet each person by introducing yourself and your relationship to the deceased: "Hi, I am Clark, and I was Jack's nephew." Shake the person's hand and ask them how they knew the deceased. If they have nothing to say or look puzzled, tell them a brief, positive story or memory about you and the deceased. If possible, tell one that includes the person with whom you are speaking (this can be really powerful). It is important to have four or five stories or memories so as to not repeat yourself over and over (that can seem a little insincere).

Let the person know that their coming to the wake is greatly appreciated and that they were an important part of the deceased's life. Make it easy for them to move down the line by introducing them to the person standing next to you. That is your job at the head of the line.

You are probably thinking right now, "Wow. That's depressing. Why did he start there?"

Looking back, if I had a starting point in dealing with my grief with Little Ronnie and had a clue of what to do, I could have been a much more supportive friend to Ron and Val rather than adding to their mountain of worries and grief. And I could have helped them through this disastrous period for their family.

In short, I could have been a better friend.

Be there for your friends first!

Part Two

In-Laws, Neighbors, and General Relationship Advice

12

Problems? What Problems?

First question: is it a problem or a fact?

My brother, John, is a calm guy and lives in Seattle.

I am high-strung and live in Boston.

I'm conservative.

He's liberal.

He's a tree lover.

I'm a tree user.

We are opposites in just about every way.

I was talking with him over the phone one day, and I noticed how calm he was. So I asked him, "Why are you always so calm? Don't you worry about anything?"

"Well," he said, "I gotta tell ya. I figured out a while ago that there are only two kinds of problems in this world."

"What are they?"

"The problems you can do something about and the problems you can't."

"That doesn't really help me much. Tell me about these two kinds of problems."

"The first are the problems I can do something about, so I do something about them. Then they're not problems, they're processes. I'm doing something about them."

"OK, I get it, but what about the ones you can't do anything about? Those are the ones that drive me crazy. What do you do about those?"

"That's the secret. The problems I can't do anything about? They're misnamed. Those aren't problems at all. Those are *facts*. When I accept them as facts, I can just move on and work on the problems I can do something about."

"Whoa!"

Shortly after that call, I was stuck in traffic.

Here in Boston, heavy traffic is a way of life. But this was unplanned and unexpected.

I started to get upset about it, but I was stuck. It was two more miles to the next exit.

So I asked myself, "Is this a problem or a fact?"

It wasn't a problem. It was a fact. There was nothing I could do about it. I couldn't turn around. I couldn't back up.

So I moved on.

I accepted the fact that I was sitting in traffic and asked myself, "What can I do instead of getting upset?" I started making calls to people I hadn't talked to in a while.

Instead of getting mad at the world and all the things over which I had no control, I reconnected with friends and clients that I hadn't spoken with in several years.

When you have a problem, the first thing to do is to ask yourself: "Is there something I can do about this, or is this a fact?"

If it's a problem that you can do something about, then do it.

Otherwise accept it as a fact, and move on. Focus your energy on things you can do something about.

First question: is it a problem or a fact?

13

The Thirty-Year Rule

Be friendly with your neighbors,
but not "besties."

My parents had a thirty-year mortgage when they bought their house.

My Dad met Jim right after we moved in. Jim lived down the street. Jim and my dad became best friends.

We played with Jim's kids. Jim and Marcia and my parents were inseparable. I mean all holidays, birthdays, family events, church events—everything.

One day Jim and Marcia disappeared off the face of the earth. They still lived down the street, but they were gone from our lives. I still saw Jim's kids at school, but since they were one and two years older, I didn't interact with them at all. They were gone.

We didn't speak about it as a family. Something happened between my dad and Jim—big-time bad. They never spoke again. I did speak with Jim at my dad's funeral forty years later. He was the organ player for the church. It was really sad. He still didn't talk about what had happened.

What's the point of this story? Just this: thank God we weren't next-door neighbors! That would have been a disaster for both families. Imagine a thirty-year mortgage keeping former best friends, now mortal enemies, locked into houses right next to each other. What a nightmare!

Best friends will fight. Most quarrels are over quickly, but some are never resolved. They can last a lifetime, like with Jim and my dad. I am sure that both men believed that they were right, whatever the issue was, but it can lead to an impossible situation if you live next door.

I love my neighbors, and I work hard to be a good neighbor. I go to all their kids' graduations and weddings. I wave hello and have pleasant conversations. They are friends, but not best friends.

The rule is, be nice to your neighbors, go to their kids' parties and graduations, and give good presents, but don't go camping with them, don't go in on a boat together, and don't do anything that might lock you into a best friend relationship. If anything goes bad, you still have to live next to them for thirty years.

Be friendly with your neighbors,
but not "besties."

14

Cookies! I Love Cookies!

Kids remember everything.

I was renting my first house in South Florida. I was mowing the lawn. A young lady in a Girl Scout uniform came up to me and asked if I would like to buy some cookies. Excitedly I said yes. I love Girl Scout cookies. Always have and always will. Now this was back in the day when it was OK to sell door-to-door.

She handed me an order sheet and I filled it out, making sure to order extras of all my favorites.

It was the first time I bought something at my own house (rented as it was), and I didn't have to get parental permission to have something delivered. I handed back the order form, and she told me that my cookies would be there in about a month.

One month later, I was mowing my lawn again, and I saw the young lady in the Girl Scout uniform walking down the street with a wheelbarrow piled high (higher than her) with boxes of cookies.

"Wow, this is great!" I thought. "She is delivering her cookies to the neighborhood." I got excited.

A few minutes later, she was at my house.

"Are you delivering all your cookie orders today?" I asked.

"Yes, I am," she smiled.

"Wow! You have a lot of cookies in your wheelbarrow. How long will it take you to deliver all of these?"

"Not long."

"You must be planning on working fast. That's a lot of cookies you have there!"

"It won't take long. These are all your cookies, Mr. Merrill. You were my biggest customer!"

I had ordered seventy boxes of Girl Scout cookies, heavy on the Thin Mints and Peanut Butter, my favorites.

Needless to say, I was the talk of the neighborhood and had made her one of the top selling Girl Scouts in town. She returned to get my order each year, until we moved up to Boston.

In hindsight, I realized that I had stumbled into one of the rules for being a harmonious neighbor: support the kids, and be a soft touch when they are fundraising!

We were always known as the generous neighbors, and we would buy anything that the kids were selling (though nothing compared with my annual Girl Scout Cookie order).

When the neighbor kids came to our house at Halloween, we gave *big* candy bars.

When we were invited to their graduation parties, weddings, bar mitzvahs, christenings, or birthdays, we gave big. Because we cared about them and wanted to be the role model neighbors as they grew up around us.

These kids are going to grow up and will remember that you were generous when they were fundraising, at Halloween, and at their parties.

Be, and be known as, the generous neighbors.

Kids remember everything.

15

Meeting New People

You have to want to!

Jim was in the waiting area of our office. I had just been promoted to director of franchising. I asked him whom he was here to see. He told me that he had an appointment with Darrlyn, the director of marketing, and that he was there to show his portfolio. He was an artist. I asked his full name.

"Jim Baldwin," he said. I told Darrlyn that he was waiting in the lobby.

Six weeks later, I saw him in the lobby again. I walked up, stuck out my hand, and said, "Good to see you again, Jim . . . Jim . . . Jim . . . Piano!"

He laughed.

"I missed it, didn't I?" I said sheepishly.

"Yes, but you were close! It's Baldwin."

I told him who I was and that I'd wanted to remember his name the first time we met. I was creating a brochure for our franchise and wanted to remember him as a future resource for this brochure. I added that the last time we met, I knew that it was important to remember his name. So I pictured him hanging from a jungle gym, playing a Baldwin piano with his toes. It was a silly picture, I admit, but I was desperate to remember his name. I worked—sort of.

I did business with Jim, and I still have his original art from that brochure hanging in my kitchen.

What was the key to remembering his name?

I had to *want to.*

In order to remember someone's name we have to turn on the *want-to.*

We really have to want to remember their names and stop thinking about ourselves.

You have to want to!

16

Ask Their Names

Remembering names can save your life!

I was rushed to the emergency room at Winchester Hospital late one Sunday night. (I mentioned this earlier. It was when Katelyn's mom, Kathy, saved my life. She stabilized me and called the ambulance.)

The ambulance driver asked my wife, Colleen, to pick Winchester Hospital because it was the closest one to our house. The driver informed Colleen that I wouldn't make it to her first choice (I found this out later).

We quickly arrived at the emergency room. I expected to leave that night, or at the very latest the next morning. I was out of touch with reality.

There was a flurry of activity around me. I was getting no information. I began to panic. I wasn't leaving anytime soon.

I had to connect with someone that could give me some information. When the ER nurse came in, I asked her name.

"Betty," she said compliantly.

I asked her how her night was going.

"Well, it's going better than yours." And she smiled. She took a deep breath and told me that I was in deep trouble, and she would catch me up when (and if) things settled down for me.

She did once I was stable, and she made sure to answer all my questions. I didn't get out for two months, but I did get to know Betty and everyone that worked there. I got to know them, and they got to know me.

Remembering names, and asking people about themselves, not only changes the environment, but builds relationships! And I didn't forget to thank everyone that came into my room for anything they did, no matter what they did or how I was feeling (sometimes this took a bit more effort and thought).

I was there for seven weeks. They saved my life. THANK YOU!

Remembering names can save your life!

17

Airport Spies

Things are rarely what they seem.

My brother and I went to Miami International Airport. It was in the seventies, back when you could go to the airport for no reason. We went because it was an adventure. We never had enough money to fly anywhere, or anywhere to fly to, for that matter, but it was fun to go to the airport and hang around. We would follow people to their gates like spies, trying not to be noticed.

My brother, John, and I didn't really get along, but on those rare occasions that we did, we would go out for breakfast. This Sunday, we decided to go to the airport for breakfast. Probably because the churches were getting out and we wanted to go somewhere with no wait, so why not take a forty-five-minute drive and pay for parking at the airport? Things like that make sense when you're seventeen.

At that time, Miami International Airport was filled with no-name stores, no-name restaurants for desperate travelers, and places where you could get the kids something from Miami because you forgot about them while you were tanning on the beach. Your penalty was to pay three times retail for everything, but if you were flying, you could afford it.

The airport was built in the fifties with the future in mind, the future being the sixties. It was a busy place, and you were just as likely to run into Muhammad Ali as you were to see a friend from high school.

There were no TSA checkpoints filled with security guards seizing your toenail clippers, no X-ray machines, no bomb sniffing dogs, no doors with alarms, no testing machines. It was an innocent place. Other than the occasional skyjacking to Cuba, not much happened.

We went to the luncheonette. That was what they called a small, informal restaurant with counter service, usually open for breakfast and lunch. We sat at the counter and ordered breakfast. The stools and counter were low, and we didn't have to face each other. We did our usual small talk and watched people coming and going from the restaurant. I envied those people. I wanted to get on a plane and be somewhere else in three hours. We talked about that. I never thought that I would ever leave Miami. John knew he would leave and was already planning his escape. He surprised all of us when he joined the Air Force.

Somewhere during the small talk, we both noticed the really attractive woman sitting directly across the bay from us. She was alone, pretty, and way out of our league. She was in her early twenties, long, straight, dirty blond hair. She was perfect, but I knew I would never have the confidence to talk to her; I was embarrassed just to be looking at her. She was obviously eating at the airport because she was a jet-setter and had no room in her life for the likes of me. She'd probably just came back from some exotic place and had a boyfriend like James Bond.

John saw her too. We looked at each other and sighed. We talked and tried not to stare. We didn't do so well. She looked sad, and we talked about that. Maybe we could cheer her up. How could such a beautiful person be sad? Surely we could cheer her up, but she would think that we were hitting on her, and we were definitely too young for her.

Oh, well. Breakfast was good, and it was a rare moment of brotherly camaraderie. As inadequate as I felt, it was a good day.

Just as we were finishing our breakfast, she stood up, really upset. We both sat there speechless, staring. She was walking right towards us; my heart was pounding. I started to fantasize.

What if she stopped and started a conversation?

What would I say?

I decided I'd be smooth: I would show her that age didn't matter.

What to say? What is smooth? Oh, God, she is coming right at us. What if she read my mind? Did she see me staring at her? What if she was coming over to tell us off? Oh crap!

I started looking for an escape route—none available. We're screwed.

Wait a minute. She'll just walk right by us. We couldn't possibly matter in her world: the world of jet travel, eating at airports. No problem; I'd just overestimated our importance to her.

All I had to do was look away and pretend that she didn't exist, as if she hadn't even noticed us. Great: I had my mind back in control. Just get the check, and leave after she was finished paying and left the area.

Just as my heart was slowing down, she was right next to us. She stopped, radiating sadness. She burst out in tears and blurted out that she didn't have any money and couldn't pay her check. Could we help?

My heart broke. My eyes welled up. I had totally misread everything. I couldn't remember being so sad for one person, ever. We both grabbed for the check and said, "No problem." She let go and hurried out of the restaurant.

I felt her embarrassment and wanted to reach out and fix her situation. I wanted to make her world right, I had no idea how. She needed help.

I stood up, and she was gone.

We looked at her check. It was for a cup of coffee and an order of toast: $1.29. I couldn't even say it was a scam. Who scams for $1.29? We went to the register and paid both checks. We went back to the counter and left two tips, $2 at our place and $2 on hers. We didn't want the waitress to think that the attractive jet-setter that she had just waited on was cheap.

We didn't talk on the way back to the car. We were stunned. Maybe my life wasn't so bad. I could afford breakfast. I could afford to help someone who couldn't.

The day was sadder; my life was better. Airport adventures would never be the same.

Things are rarely what they seem.

18

A Kiss Is Just a Kiss, but a Case of Kisses Lasts Forever

Make your commitments to kids extra special.

When my niece, Katelyn, was a little girl, she had a major sweet tooth. (She still does!) My wife, Colleen, owned a restaurant, so we used to go to supply houses to get different things. There was a supply house for candy close to us. A huge warehouse of candy!

When Katelyn was five, Colleen asked her if she wanted to go to the store. Of course she wanted to go; she'd go anywhere with Colleen. So we went to the candy warehouse. It was a big brown building, no windows. You couldn't tell it was a candy warehouse from the outside.

We walked in, and Katelyn's eyes lit up. We went into the tasting room, where we could sample the candies. We tried a couple (Katelyn and I stuffed our faces). Then Colleen said to her, "Let's go out into the warehouse, and you can buy whatever you want."

"Really?!" Katelyn shouted.

We went out into the warehouse, and Katelyn was picking one or two things out of each box.

I leaned down to her and said, "Katelyn, you know, Colleen said you could buy whatever you want. If you like the candy, why not get the whole box, get the whole case?"

She said, "Really?"

I said, "Yes. I'll put it up at the front."

Katelyn was *the* little kid in a candy shop. (Actually, this was a candy warehouse.) She pointed out the boxes, and I brought them to the front and piled them up. She ended up with five cases of candy, jelly beans, gummy bears, and chocolate, and these were pretty big cases.

They asked if we needed them delivered.

Colleen asked Katelyn. She said, "I'll take them now!"

We went to the car. Katelyn sat in the back seat. We strapped her in and put all the boxes of candy next to her. (She didn't want them in the trunk.)

She was excited.

To this day, her mom is still trying to think of ways to thank us.

We didn't have kids (by choice), so we decided to become the best aunt and uncle on the planet. We made a commitment that whenever we were around our nieces and nephews, whatever they wanted, we would, to the best of our ability, get for them.

We didn't want to be those adults that made promises to kids and never kept them. If you think back in your memory, I'm sure you can remember times when somebody made a promise to you as a kid and never followed through, because they forgot or because they didn't think it was important.

Kids are important. The relationship you have with kids when they're younger sets a relationship that you're going to have with them for the rest of their lives. So make a commitment, and keep it.

Make your commitments to kids extra special.

19

Life Is a Party!

*Make everyone's time with you
an exceptional experience.*

It was Katelyn's sixteenth birthday. She wanted to have a Sweet Sixteen party and invite all her friends. She asked Colleen if she could have it at our house.

"Of course!" Colleen said. We have a big house with a good-sized backyard.

"How many friends can I bring over?" Katelyn asked.

"Bring them all over. Just tell me how many, so we can make the food and make sure they have a great time."

So Katelyn invited all of her friends, about twenty-five of them.

They didn't know what to expect. When they came into the backyard, they found a sixteen-year-old's dreamland—with food, snacks, and music, and decorated to the hilt.

Hanging from the tree was a piñata. It was donkey-shaped. The kids all thought it was filled with candy, since that was Katelyn's favorite food source.

They each took turns blindly swinging at it, but there was a lack of enthusiasm. There were already tons of candy lying around, so they didn't see the point of having even more flying around after a successful swing,

It took a while, but blindfolded determination finally paid off. But instead of candy, the piñata was crammed full with makeup—really good makeup. A sixteen-year-old girl's dream. It was unbelievable.

The girls went nuts! They dove on the ground, grabbing the makeup, and then they started laughing. Colleen made sure that there was plenty for everyone. The rest of the party went the same way. They really had a great time, and it's one of those parties that has been remembered not only by Katelyn, but by all of her friends.

This was not the exception at our house; it was the rule. It was always about the guest. Whether for one hour or two weeks, it was about making their time with us exceptional.

Having a party is for the people that are attending it, not for the people that are throwing it. If you think about what your guests want and create a party around that, they're going to have a great time, but more importantly, they're going to remember it.

*Make everyone's time with you
an exceptional experience.*

20

Joey Bag-o'-Donuts and the Worldview

The world is full of good people doing good work.

Scotty was a coworker.

"There he is again!"

"Who?"

"Joey Bag-o'-Donuts!"

"Who is that?"

"That homeless guy outside the window. Every day about this time, he walks by eating a bag of donuts."

"How do you know he's homeless?"

"I don't. I just guess by the way he looks and the way he walks."

I never realized it before, but I viewed the world the same way Scotty did. He was just vocal about it.

I paused and thought about what I had just heard.

How do you see the world? There's positive, there's negative, there's optimistic, and then there's critical. I was critical. Maybe because of my life experiences. Maybe genetics. Maybe who knows. The more I thought about it, the bigger the hole I saw developing in my worldview.

It really comes down to how I view people. There are good people; there are bad people. Now of course I know there are bad people in the world, and there's nothing I can do about it. But if I go around thinking that everybody's bad and everybody's out to get me, it makes me cynical and untrusting.

I realized that if I saw everyone that was different from me like my coworker—as just a Joey Bag-o'-Donuts—that would limit the relationships and connections that I could build.

I made a choice. I sat down and said, "All right, from now on, this is a world filled with good people doing good work. Period! Even Joey Bag-o'-Donuts. I know there are bad people, but I'm gonna assume that everybody's a good person, and they're doing good work."

It took me a couple of months. Every time I saw someone walking, I said, "There's a good person doing good work."

What happened?

My mindset shifted. I opened up and started to meet new people. My first assumption was that they were good people doing good things. If they weren't, I would deal with it later.

So some question to ask are, "How am I viewing people? Are they good people doing good work, or are they out to get me?"

Those who are out to get us are few and far between. So make your mind up about how you are going to view people. You know there are good people doing good work and good things. Or is there some great conspiracy going on where everybody in the world is out to get us? I'm inclined to go with the first option. Even Joey, the person my coworker looked for every day out the window, is an excellent person doing excellent things.

The world is full of good people doing good work.

21

Saving the Lawn Mower

A little VISION goes a long way.

The first house we bought had a big yard. There were lots of half-buried rocks in the yard. It was a new house, and the builder did not care about the yard.

I would run over the half-buried rocks with my lawn mower and make big sparks. Cool to see. Not cool for my lawn mower. It was annoying. I kept hitting them even though I tried to avoid them.

So one Saturday I got up early and said, "All right, I have to do something about this."

I had a vision of mowing the lawn without hitting any rocks.

I got my wheelbarrow, a shovel, and a pick, and I started digging out rocks one by one and moving them to an old stone wall in my backyard. I was doing pretty well.

Now these were big rocks. I got them all except the last one in the front yard; it was sticking up, and I'd hit it a bunch of times. As I started to dig around it, the rock got bigger and bigger and bigger. My testosterone was kicking in. I kept digging. "I'm going to get this rock, and this rock isn't going to beat me."

So I dug and dug around it. This rock was three and a half feet wide and two feet down. I kept digging and finally started digging under it.

Then I got under it! The rock was loose!

But now how would I get it out of the hole? I still hadn't won.

I went back to the garage and found some two-by-fours. I came back to the hole and used the two-by-fours as levers to lift the massive rock out. It took a while, but I finally rolled it out of the hole.

Now there was this big rock sitting in the middle of my front yard next to a big hole. Not pretty.

I was feeling proud. I got the rock out. I felt accomplished! "I can do anything!"

Then it dawned on me. What was I going to do with it?

It was way too heavy for me to lift. Even if I got all my neighbors to help put the rock in my wheelbarrow, it would crush it. It wasn't the kind of rock that was easy to roll. It was one of those oddly shaped stones the glaciers dropped off in my front yard 15,000 years ago. What was I going to do with it?

My pride of accomplishment turned to frustration. I now had a bigger problem than when I started.

I went into the house and got a glass of lemonade. It was a hot summer day. I came out and sat on the rock, looking down at the hole, thinking about my predicament.

What was I going to do with this rock?

My vision had been to mow the lawn without hitting the rocks, and now I had a bigger rock disposal problem on my hands.

Bingo! It hit me. My initial vision was to mow the lawn without hitting any rocks, not to collect as many rocks as I could and pile them in my backyard.

I didn't need to move the rock! I needed to dig the hole deeper so I could bury the rock and it wouldn't be sticking out above the ground.

So I started digging. I dug extra deep, because there was no way I was taking this rock out of the hole again.

I took that rock and my two-by-four lever, and I rolled it back into the hole. I took the dirt and filled in the rest of the hole.

Problem solved.

Let's talk about the power of a vision. We know we have to have a vision for life, even though most of us don't.

Companies have visions. Teams have visions. Visions allow us to make decisions and move forward in a direction where we want to go.

That's the power of a vision. I knew what I wanted to have happen, and having a vision helped me find a new way to solve the problems that cropped up. I didn't have to move the rock, just to put it in a deeper hole.

Even with little projects, ask yourself before you start what your vision is: "When I get done here, what's it going to look like?" It can help you get rid of the rocks in your heart, and even the ones in your head.

A little VISION goes a long way.

22

The Trip to Nowhere

There is power in letting go from time to time.

I'm the kind of guy who is very organized.

I like to have things planned.

If I travel, I want to know where I'm going. Who's going to meet me, where I'm going to stay, what car I'm going to drive.

While I think that's a very good way to lead my life, it can also be very limiting.

Colleen was serendipitous. She did things because she thought they were good to do.

I came home from work and Colleen said, "Clark, pack a bag."

"Pack a bag? Where are we going?"

"It doesn't matter. Just pack your bag."

I was skeptical. "Is it someplace warm or cool?"

"It's not warm or cool. Just pack your bag."

I loved her, so I trusted her. I started packing.

Colleen called our friend Lisa, and I heard her telling Lisa the same thing. "Pack a bag. We're going to come pick you up and go to the airport."

We got to the airport and asked Colleen, "Where are we going?"

"I don't know!"

She walked up to the ticket counter and asked the ticket agent what planes were flying out this afternoon.

The ticket agent looked at her and said, "We have a flight to Utah. We have a flight to California. We have a flight to Fort Lauderdale."

We live in Boston, so Fort Lauderdale sounded pretty good. "When's the flight to Fort Lauderdale leaving?"

Colleen bought three tickets from Boston to Fort Lauderdale. She came back and told us where we were going. The flight was in about an hour, and although we didn't get seats together, we were close enough.

"But where are we staying?" I asked.

Colleen went back to the ticket agent and said, "Thank you so much for your help. We're going to Fort Lauderdale. Do you know any good places to stay?"

The ticket agent's face lit up. "I go down there all the time!" She went into her personal file and gave Colleen the name and number of the hotel she stays at.

Colleen called and booked our hotel. She did the same thing with a car rental agency.

We got on the plane and had a great flight down to Fort Lauderdale. We took a cab to the car rental agency and picked up the rental car. It was a midsized car, and I'm a big guy. I fit like a size twelve foot into a size five shoe.

"This isn't going to work," I said. I started to go negative.

"I'll be right back." Colleen went inside the agency, talked to the agent, and came back with another set of keys. She pointed to a big Cadillac and said, "This is our car." She got it for the same price as the smaller car! The agent was a big guy too.

We got to the hotel. It was amazing. It had a pool with a lagoon. You could walk right from the hotel on the beach. Beautiful, beautiful sand. It was great.

We were there for four days when Colleen said, "Hey, let's go to Key West. I've never been."

We didn't have a hotel, but I didn't question any-thing—just went with the flow. My mom lived south of Miami, so I called her up and said, "Hey, Mom, do you want to go to Key West?" She did, and we picked her up about an hour and ten minutes later.

The four of us were in this great big Cadillac, driving down to Key West over the seven-mile bridge, and it was beautiful. But now I was worried that we didn't have a place to stay in Key West, and finding a hotel if you don't have a reservation can be tough.

As we drove, we were on the ocean side of Key West, and there was a big building with no windows that said "Marriott."

Colleen said, "Pull into here." She went in and fifteen minutes later came out with a suite.

"How much is that going to cost?" I asked.

"It's going to cost us the same as if we just got a room."

I was shocked. "How did you do that?"

"I gave him my business card. He opened up a business account and was able to get the room at the off-season business rate."

We weren't off-season. But Colleen was amazing, believing that things would work out if we could just get out of their way.

We ended up having a great time. We saw the Key West sunset and had great food and an awesome time.

That's the power of serendipity. You have to throw up your hands, say, "What the heck," and have a good time, trusting that it's all going to work out.

Put some serendipity in your life, and see what happens.

There is power in letting go from time to time.

23

Take Care of Your Friends

*Success is about making everyone
around us successful.*

At the beginning of one of our weekly science tutoring sessions, Katelyn handed me a copy of the periodic table.

"What is this for?" I asked.

"I have to memorize the first three lines."

"Why?"

"I don't know."

"Well, first off, you've got to ask your teacher why. Don't ever do something if you don't know the why behind it. But let's see what we can do with this."

Rote memorization can be tough. We all had to do it with spelling, the multiplication tables, and other painful things. It's not fun, and for most of us, not easy.

One of the first nights Katelyn and I worked together, she told me she wasn't smart.

"Oh, you're smart. You just think differently. I bet you know the thirteen colonies and the order they came into the Union, right?"

"What? You're crazy!"

"If I could teach you that, would you think you were smart?"

"Sure."

So I taught her a mnemonic device for remembering the thirteen original colonies in the order in which they ratified the Constitution. It was kind of a story, and by the end she knew the story and the thirteen colonies.

Now back to the periodic table.

I said, "Do you remember the whole thing about colonies?"

"Yes."

"Let's do the same thing with the periodic table."

So we made up a story about a rabbit, Benjamin Bunny, going out on the town. It went something like this: **H**iding, **HE Li**t a cigar for his friend **Beryl**. **Boron**, his brother, got **Carbon** ashes all over his new suit. It was a **NIT** suit. You get the idea.

We finished the story. She wrote down the story as we came up with it. I handed her another piece of paper and told her to write the story four times. Then I gave her a blank piece of paper and told her to write it down again. And again. And again. And again.

"So here's the deal. When you take your science test, write this story on the top of the page. If your teacher gives you any grief, tell her it's none of her business. Give me a call, and I'll come to the school and take care of it for you."

Next week she arrived, and I asked, "How'd it go on the test?"

"We all got a hundred."

"We *all*?"

"Yes, we *all*. I taught my friends the story and told them to write it on the top of the test paper. I told them that if the teacher said anything to tell me and that I would call you to come and fix it. They did, and we all got a hundred."

I was stunned.

"You know really smart people in school, don't you?" I said. "What do you think they would have done if they had this information before a test?"

"They would have kept it to themselves so that they could look smart."

"You see? Someday people like that are going to be working for you. You took care of your friends. That's what bosses do. That's what leaders do. They take care of the people around them. They make them successful. I told you when we started this science thing that you think differently. This is why I said that. You think like a leader."

Later on, when Katelyn was applying for college and couldn't think of a topic for her essay, I reminded her of this story. Colleges are always looking for leaders.

It worked. She was accepted to three colleges, got her degree in business administration, and is planning to get her master's degree in business.

Success is about making everyone around us successful.

24

Coffee and a Prize Fight

What's the prize?

My Uncle Jack and his girlfriend, Edith, lived in a house on Belle Isle Marsh in Revere, Massachusetts, just north of Boston. Every once in a while on Sunday mornings, I'd stop off at Dunkin' Donuts, pick up some coffees, and go over there. He had a great deck, with a view of the Boston skyline over the marsh. We would watch the sun come up.

One day I was there, sitting in the kitchen, drinking coffee with Jack. Edith was in the bathroom, getting ready for their day. Edith mentioned that they were closing the Chelsea Street Bridge next week for the annual fair.

Jack corrected her. "No Edith, that's in two weeks."

"No, Jack, I'm sure it's next Saturday."

"It's in two weeks. I talked to the person who is setting it up."

"No, I read it in the paper, and the paper said next week."

Now I started to see the argument escalating. It was like a tennis match going back and forth.

"It's next week."

"No, it's in two weeks."

Sitting there with my coffee, I raised my hand. Jack saw me and was a little annoyed.

"Jack? I have a question to ask." I said.

"What? What's your question?"

"Let's suppose just for giggles, that there is a Federal Bureau of Arguments. They've listened, and they've decided that you won this argument. Hands down, no doubt about it! They hand you a certificate stating that you have absolutely won this argument."

He smiles, "Yeah."

"Jack? What do you win?"

"What do you mean, 'What do I win?'"

"You have won. What do you win? What is your prize?

Is Edith going to get excited and say, 'Let me give you a big hug'? Will she declare it Jack Appreciation Day all day? Is she going to throw you a party for winning? What exactly is the prize you are fighting for?"

Long pause.

"Yeah, I guess you're right. There is no prize."

He then turned to Edith and said, "Clark's right. There's no prize here. I'm sorry I started this argument."

Edith replied, "Oh no, I'm sorry. It was silly. I'm the one who started the argument."

"No, Edith, I started it!"

"No, Jack, I'm sorry! I started it!"

It was kind of funny, but the reality is that the difference between a disagreement and an argument is the emotion. You can disagree all you want if you're not emotional about it, because your emotional brain won't have the urge to say stupid things.

When the emotion kicks in, it's probably time to stop and ask the question, "If I win this, what's the prize?" If there is a prize, then tell the other person: "Here is why we're going to have this argument, because this is what I want, and this is the prize that I am fighting for." At least they will know what's at stake.

They might not care and concede. They might be fighting for something else entirely, which you might not care about. But if there is no prize, you realize that maybe you're fighting for nothing.

Honestly, that's eliminated 80 percent of the emotional arguments that I have. I still have them, but at least both sides know what we are fighting for and we've set the ground rules.

So whenever you feel an argument starting and the emotions are kicking in, stop and ask yourself, "What's the prize?"

What's the prize?

25

First Movie

Kids make great investments.

When my nephew Greg was little, he was different from my other nieces and nephews. The first time I really got to know him, he was about two years old, and we were having a big party at our house. He was knocking things off the coffee table and knocking over chairs. I was always saying, "Greg, put this down," and "Greg, back away" throughout the whole party.

As he was leaving, I said, "Hey, Greg, aren't you going to say goodbye?" He turned around, gave me this look, and kept walking.

His mother, Sherry, said, "You know, Clark, he's not stupid. He knows when people don't like him." This broke my heart. I realized that I had been a real jerk to this little kid. So I turned to Colleen and said,

"You know what? I want to make a difference in that kid's life."

She looked at me and said, "If you start this, don't back off. You can't back off on this. This isn't going to be a halfway thing."

"OK," I said.

A couple of weeks later, we were having a family dinner at a restaurant with all of Colleen's family. I said to Greg, "Hey, Greg, why don't you come over here and sit next to me?" He looked at me, and I said, "No, really. Come on over here and sit; it might be fun." So he did.

He ended up sitting in my lap so I could help him order. The waiter came over and pointed to a children's menu, but Greg saw the prime rib on the adult menu.

"What do you want to eat, Greg?" I asked.

He pointed to the prime rib.

"OK, we'll get you the prime rib."

His mother looked at me. I told her, "I got this. I'll pay for it."

The food came, and I helped him cut his prime rib. He accidentally knocked his Coke over. Everyone started to get upset. There were fifteen or twenty people there, and Greg started to get upset too, because he thought he was going to get in trouble.

I started laughing. "Greg, don't worry about it, buddy." I grabbed a handful of napkins and started cleaning it up. We both laughed as everyone watched. That's when I started to build the relationship with him.

At the end of the dinner, I said, "Hey, Greg, do you want to go to the movies?"

His face lit up. "Yeah!"

"Ask your mom if it's OK."

"Can I go to the movies with Clark?"

His mom said yes, and I offered to bring his brothers or have it just be the two of us; it was up to Greg. He chose just the two of us.

The next week, he picked a movie. I picked him up at his house, strapped him in the car, and off we went to the movies.

We arrived, and I asked, "Do you want candy?"

Of course he wanted candy. So we went to the candy counter. The place was mobbed, and the lines were long. We finally got up to the front, and a young girl asked, "Can I help you?"

I pointed down to Greg and said, "Get him whatever he wants."

Then he disappeared! I started to freak out. Where could he have gone? He had moved to a counter where he could see and point to the candy.

The girl at the counter caught up to us and asked what he wanted. He pointed through the glass and said, "I'll have one of those, and one of those, and one of those, and one of those . . ."

I was seeing a future where Greg was eating all that candy and getting sick. Not a good thing, but I did say he could have anything he wanted.

Finally he said, "And I want a cherry Slurpee."

I paid for everything, and we headed into the theater, with Greg balancing all the candy in his arms, the cherry Slurpee in his right hand.

"You know, Greg, you can have whatever you want, but if you eat all that candy and get sick, your mom might not let us go to the movies again."

He looked up at me and said, "These aren't for me."

"What do you mean they're not for you?"

"Well, this is for my brother Sean. This is for my brother Brian. This is for my mom. This is for my dad, this for my brother Pete."

My eyes started to well up with tears.

"What are you having?"

"I'm having the cherry Slurpee."

I realized why I'd made the choice to invest my time with this kid: he was going to teach me so much. And he did. We went to the movies and did a lot of other things. Now he's twenty-eight, has an amazing job, and is living a great life. He is still the most generous person I have ever known!

Kids make great investments.

Part Three

❋

Money, Career, and General Life Advice

❋

26

Talking in the Morning Always Helps

Find the right person, find the right job.

It was 4:30 in the morning. I was getting ready to go to work. I had to let the baker in. I was shaving in the mirror.

Out loud I said: "I hate this job! I really hate this job!"

I shaved a little and stared in the mirror.

"How much would they have to pay me to like this job?

"Another $25,000?

"I'd still hate it!

"$50,000?

"Still hate it!

"$100,000?

"Nope! I would hate this job if they paid me $1 million!"

I ended the conversation with myself, got dressed, and went to work.

At dinner that evening Colleen asked me, "Who were you talking to in the bathroom this morning?"

A little embarrassed, I said, "Nobody. I was just a little upset, and I was verbalizing."

"Upset about what?"

"My job. I know we have a mortgage to pay, so I'll just do what I have to do."

"Well, if you could do anything in the world, what would you do?"

I thought about it and said, "I would teach the leadership and relationship class that I deliver once a week for Kevin."

I was a contract trainer for a company and had worked very hard to develop some competence in delivering their program. I absolutely loved doing it.

"Well, then, why don't you do that?"

"Because they don't have full-time trainers."

"Call your friend Kevin right now."

Kevin was my friend who gave me these classes to teach when they came up.

"Why?"

"Just call him."

I dialed his number.

"Hello."

"Hi, Kev, this is Clark. Colleen told me to call you."

"Why?"

"I don't know."

"Ask her."

"Why did you want me to call Kevin?"

"Ask him if we can buy him dinner tomorrow night."

"She wants to know if we can buy you dinner tomorrow night."

"Sure. I have a meeting. How about 9:00 at Bertucci's?"

"Ok. We'll see you then."

We arrived at Bertucci's, got a table, ordered drinks, and waited for Kevin. He arrived shortly after 9:00 and joined us.

"What's up?" he asked.

"I don't know."

"Tell him the conversation you had with yourself yesterday morning in the bathroom," Colleen said.

More than a little embarrassed, I did, salary numbers and all.

"She asked me what I wanted to do if I could do any job, so I told her I would love to work for you full-time, but you don't have any full-time trainers. So I don't know why we are here."

"Hmmm . . . That's interesting. We were talking about bringing on a full-time trainer last month. The business has really grown, and we need someone full-time."

"Damn. Why didn't you call me?"

"Clark, there's no way can we afford you! You are really good, but this job is way below your salary league."

Just then Colleen took out a pen and scribbled something on her cocktail napkin. She folded it in half and slid it over to Kevin.

"Can you afford this?" she said.

Kevin picked up the napkin and looked at what was on it. I was a genuinely uninformed bystander at this point.

"Will he work for this?"

"It's a one-time offer. No negotiating. That is the minimum we can afford," she said.

"I think we can make this work. I'll let you know in a couple of weeks."

I had no idea of what had just happened. We ordered dinner and talked about everything in the world except what was written on that cocktail napkin. Colleen picked up the check, and we said good night to Kevin.

In the car I asked what was on the napkin.

"It doesn't matter." she said.

"It does to me!"

"Listen, ever since you've had your job, you've been awful to live with, except for that one night a week when you are teaching for Kevin. Put a price on that!"

Three weeks later, Kevin called and told me that I got the job. I gave my notice and started two months later.

I didn't find out what was on that napkin until I opened my first paycheck. I cried. It was low. But I have to say that since my first day on this job I have not "worked" a single day! Colleen was right: I love this job and can't imagine doing anything else.

We got by on that salary, I grew in the job, and things got better.

I wasn't sure where to place this story in this book. I placed it in this section because it's about finding the right job for yourself—and there *is* a right job out there for you.

But I think it really belongs in the relationship section. What Colleen did was based on love and sacrifice. She did this for me so that we would have a better life together. We did have an amazing life because of her!

Find the right person, find the right job.

27

Ask Questions and Be Humble

*There is always someone that
knows how to do what you don't.*

Calvin Coolidge once said, "Nobody ever listened their way out of a job." It was true then, it's true today, and it will be true a hundred years from now.

I left my job at Hickory Farms of Ohio in Miami to take a position at Brigham's restaurant chain in Arlington, Massachusetts. I was to be fast-tracked into their middle management, but first I had to learn the day-to-day store operations as a manager trainee and eventually work up to store manager.

Brigham's was an ice cream place, but I knew nothing about ice cream or the company's operating systems. I had a choice. I could assume that I knew most of what I needed and bullshit my way through the rest, or I could listen to everything they said, be humble, and keep my mouth shut. The first would be easy and would fit my personality. The second would be very challenging.

I knew that Bernie, the director of operations, had taken a huge risk in hiring me. I also knew that when you start a new job, it's important that the person that hired you looks good. They are the one taking the risk, and as a new hire, it's up to you to make them look like a superstar.

So I sucked it up, listened, watched, and asked a lot of questions, most good, some stupid, but I asked. I worked hard at every position and eventually got the hang of it. I earned respect from all the staff and other managers because I would try anything and was not afraid to ask questions. I thanked everyone I worked with.

It's important that when you come across something new and unknown, don't try to fake it. Don't BS it. If you don't know what's going on, ask someone. Be candid. Ask for help.

Candor is the antithesis of arrogance. If you don't know what you're doing and guess and get it wrong, you're just going to make a lot of extra work for a lot of people.

Each time I moved to a new restaurant, the first thing I did was watch and keep my mouth shut. I did this for the first two weeks. I asked a lot of questions.

"Where does this go? Where does that go? Why are we putting it here?"

I'd rather be a little bit annoying by asking too many questions than be really annoying by assuming I knew the answer and then messing up.

Also, by asking someone who might end up working for me, I showed them that I was the kind of person who listens and just might be a good boss someday.

Listening is a key skill. Ask questions and be humble. Who knows? You might even find a mentor who can help you navigate the whole thing and help you become really successful.

Listen; ask questions. Honesty and candor are the foundation for building a trusting team.

There is always someone that knows how to do what you don't.

28

If You Could Only Shut Up!

Remember the six-second rule and SKYMS.

When I was growing up, my mother told me that I had some good things to say, but I just didn't know when to shut up.

"If I just knew when to keep my mouth shut, your life would be much easier!" she said.

In fact, *her* life would be much easier.

This was reiterated to me by my mentor, David, as he was coaching me to become part of middle management in New England. At the time he just said, "Clark, instead of talking, if you just smile and keep your mouth shut and listen, then you're gonna save yourself a lot of grief."

I took that to heart. When I went to meetings, I had his advice written across the top of my pad, using these letters: SKYMS, which stands for "Smile; keep your mouth shut."

Colleen saw this on my notes and asked me, "What is that? What does that mean?"

I said, "It's to remind me to smile and keep my mouth shut."

On her own, she went to a jeweler, had a silver ring made for me with the initials SKYMS on it, and told me to wear it where I could read it. She pointed to it often, especially at family events.

Now this works great by itself, but it's especially powerful when combined with the six-second rule.

The six-second rule is this: when you feel an emotional urge to say something, *stop talking* for six seconds!

Six seconds is the minimum amount of time needed to give the brain a chance to come up with an alternative to saying or doing something other than the immediate, emotional thing to say or do.

So when somebody says something, perhaps trying to push my buttons, the first thing I do is stop talking for six seconds.

I stop and count 1,001, 1,002, 1,003, 1,004, all the way up to 1,006. That is critical.

In that time, the brain comes up with alternative courses of action, sometimes two or three. Sometimes it just says, "It's not worth it." When that happens, I don't do or say anything.

That six seconds helps me avoid countless career limiting and career ending opportunities.

But the six-second rule doesn't work unless you smile and keep your mouth shut.

The next time someone pushes your buttons and you feel the urge to say something, stop, smile, keep your mouth shut, and count for six seconds. Trust that your brain will come up with something that is more appropriate than what you want to blurt out instantaneously.

Remember the six-second rule and SKYMS.

29

"Four Raspberry Lime Rickeys, Please"

Talk to the people around you. Make their lives a little better every time you can.

It was Wednesday, the day before Thanksgiving, and I was in my wife's restaurant.

I was sitting at the counter and having lunch. She came and sat next to me. We were talking and having lunch together.

She was watching her store from the counter. She could see how the store was operating. If there were any problems, people would come to her. But when we were eating together, they pretty much left us alone.

While we were there, an older gentleman came up to the counter and ordered. It was busy, and I couldn't hear what he was saying.

Colleen was watching the person behind the counter as they started making his order for him.

"I'll be right back," she said, and when she got up, she went behind the counter.

She headed for the back room. She was gone for about two minutes. When she returned, she had two large paper bags. She walked to the customer at the counter. They had a brief conversation. I couldn't hear what they were saying.

She handed the customer the two bags, and I could see him get emotional. She came back and sat down next to me. She didn't say a word.

I turned to her and said, "Who was that?"

"Oh, it's a new customer."

"What's his name?"

"I don't know."

"What did you talk to him about?"

"Well, he's been coming in for about two and a half, three weeks, every day at this time. And he orders four raspberry lime rickeys."

For those of you that aren't familiar with New England and don't know what a raspberry lime rickey is, it's two ounces of raspberry syrup and a whole lime cut in quarters, which you squeeze into a twenty-four-ounce cup. Fill to the top with ice and soda water, and stir. It's really good. It's the most refreshing summer drink.

Colleen told me that the customer ordered four raspberry lime rickeys every day about that time.

One day she was talking with him and asked what brought him here and why he ordered the four raspberry lime rickeys every day.

He said his wife was in the hospital up the street. She had stage four cancer and was going through chemotherapy. The rickeys were the only thing she could keep down after chemo.

"OK. What was in the bag?"

She said, "Tomorrow is Thanksgiving, and we're closed. So I put a quart of raspberry syrup, one of our lime squeezers, a dozen limes, four quart bottles of soda water, a stack of cups and lids, and napkins and straws in the bag. I wrote the recipe for making raspberry lime rickeys on an index card and put it in the bag too. I handed him the bags and told him that we were going to be closed tomorrow. He was disappointed."

"But don't worry," she told him. "Everything is here to make your own raspberry lime rickeys for your wife. All you need to do is ask the hospital for some ice."

That's when his tears welled up.

I knew why he got so emotional, because I got emotional too.

Every day I say to myself, "Man, if I could be 10 percent of the person she was, I would be 1000 percent better than I am right now."

Know the people around you, and take care of the world. And perhaps the world will take care of you.

Talk to the people around you. Make their lives a little better every time you can.

30

You Can Always Get More Stuff

Stuff is replaceable. Time is gone forever!

My sister, Dottie Sue, was nine years younger than me. I was the oldest; she was the youngest. We became close for a lot of different reasons. We spoke often even though we were 1,500 miles apart. She lived in Fort Lauderdale, and I lived in Boston.

Once she called me, really upset.

"What's the matter?" I asked.

"I'm breaking up, and I want to get my stuff out of the apartment, but the lock was changed! I don't know what I'm going to do." She started going off on a tirade.

I let her go on for a couple of minutes. Then I stopped her. "OK, let's take the next fifteen minutes. You can tell me everything that's wrong, and then we'll see if we can come up with some answers."

For the next fifteen minutes, she did. She started off: "I don't have my records or my pillows. It's my furniture: I paid for it!" The longer the list got, the louder and madder she became.

She just kept going. I listened intently, asking her questions to be sure that she listed everything. I gave her a time count: ten minutes, five minutes, two minutes—TIME!

She stopped and took a deep breath.

"Do you feel a little better?"

"Yes."

"OK, so let's do an inventory here. What are all the things you can't get out of the apartment?"

She started listing things.

I interrupted, asking, "Are you physically hurt?"

"No."

"OK, so we have the basics. That's all we need. What's in the apartment is just stuff. You came out, and you're healthy. You're not hurt. Nothing else matters.

"We can get more stuff. Eventually you'll have way more stuff than you want, so this is helping you get rid of some of the extra stuff in advance.

"More importantly, you're getting rid of the thing you need to get rid of, which is an unhealthy relationship.

"So if you want me to send you boxes of stuff or if you need some money to get you through, I'll send it to you, but write off your stuff, because if it's keeping you upset, that's their way of controlling you.

"Let go of the stuff, for crying out loud, and send me a list. I'll mail you some stuff."

She started chuckling. "Yeah, you're right."

"You're in a lot better place, even if you just have your car. If you need a place to live, just let me know. I will help you out. It's just stuff. You can always get more stuff."

Stuff is replaceable. Time is gone forever!

31

The Magic Is at the End

Appreciation creates its own kind of magic.

Twenty-five years ago, I got together with some friends, and we decided to have a night on the town and see a show. It was a magic show, Penn and Teller, playing in Boston. Now I love magic. I don't understand it, but I love it. Eight of us went to the show. It was phenomenal.

One of the things I love about Penn and Teller is that at the end of the show, they sign autographs. A lot of times when you go to shows, the stars aren't available, or they charge for the autograph. Not these guys. So I decided to stand in line and have them sign my program.

I rushed downstairs and got in Teller's line first. Now, if you're not familiar with them, Teller doesn't talk. Teller is silent. Penn does all the talking. I noticed that when people got up to him for the autograph, he signed but didn't talk. If someone asked a question, he just nodded and smiled.

A year earlier, Teller did a piece for National Public Radio about carnivals, carnies, and the shows they put on. It was an amazing and touching comparison between the carnival shows, the presenters, and his and Penn's show.

As he was signing my program, I told Teller how much I enjoyed hearing him on NPR. I told him that I hoped he would do more of that kind of radio, because it was really awesome.

He slowed down his signing, looked up, smiled, and handed the autographed program back. I walked away. I was about seven feet away. He looked towards me and said, "Hey, did you really like it?"

I turned around and I said, "I loved it. Please do more!"

He said, "Thank you so much."

Then, smiling, he turned around and kept signing autographs, but didn't speak with anyone else that I noticed.

Let people know when you really appreciate what they did, especially when they go outside of their norm and have an impact on you.

Appreciation creates its own kind of magic.

32

Bucket List or Not, This Is Hard!

You are the only one that controls what you are thinking.

It was a hot summer night. I was taking my fourth martial arts class, and there were twenty adults in the room. We had just completed a horrific warm-up. It was brutal. I was gasping for breath.

Now it was time to move on to practice the night's form. The head instructor called me over. Obediently I went over and did my white-belt bow. I was just barely holding it together.

When I was forty-two, I decided that one of my bucket list items was to get a black belt in martial arts. My best friend, Kevin, was doing martial arts and loved it, so I signed up.

It took me ten years, but I did get a black belt. This lesson, my fourth, was one of the most memorable experiences.

"Clark," the instructor asked, "what's on your mind right now?"

I paused and took a deep breath. "Surviving," I said. "I don't know if I'm going to make it to the end of the class."

"I understand whenever you come into this training room, you will always have the same two choices," he said.

"Your first choice is, you can choose to survive. If you choose to survive, you will survive. I haven't lost anyone yet. And you're not going to be the first.

"Your second choice is, you can choose to grow. When you make that choice, while you're here working with me and the other instructors, perhaps on your way home, you'll be amazed at what you did that you never thought was possible.

"But the choice is yours."

I got it.

Ever since that lesson, whenever I get stressed, I ask myself, "Do I just want to survive, or do I want to grow? Do I want to learn something from this? Or do I just want to get through it?"

They're both valid choices. Sometimes it is just a matter of surviving. But quite often it's a growth thing. What can I learn here? Every time I take that approach, I have a whole new mindset. It allows me to walk away from the experience, even if I was less than successful, and say, "Here's what I learned that I didn't know before."

So in these situations, ask yourself, are you just trying to survive, or is this an opportunity to grow?

You are the only one that controls what you are thinking.

33

The Price of Cool

Your mom is always watching.

I grew up in Cutler Ridge, Florida (now Cutler Bay, although there is no bay anywhere around, and certainly not one named "Cutler"). It was your basic middle-class neighborhood, a neighborhood where every third house looked the same. Not a bad place to grow up.

When I was thirteen, we got a new next-door neighbor. It was a single mom and her son, Bucky. Bucky was a year or a year and a half older than me. He was one of the cool guys—riding motorcycles with his friends, hanging out, and getting into trouble. Not me. I wasn't cool like he was. He only had his mom. I had two parents. He was able to get away with a lot more stuff. He was cool.

Three years later, Bucky was seventeen and was trying to buy a motorcycle that didn't have a clear title. He needed to get that title notarized in order to register it.

My mom happened to be a notary public. Bucky came over to ask her to notarize the title. She looked at it and said no. He tried to talk her into it, but she was very adamant, with a nice but firm "No."

Bucky really wanted this bike. So he came up with another plan. He saw me on my front porch and asked me, "Can you do me a little favor?"

"What?" It was cool that he was asking *me* for a favor!

"Just grab the notary seal from your mom's desk. We can notarize this title, and then I'll get the motorcycle. It'll be cool. Nobody will know."

This was my big chance to be cool and get into the group that I'd been wanting to be part of for years, not just in my neighborhood, but at school. This was my chance to create a real identity.

All I had to do was to borrow my mom's notary seal and help Bucky get his motorcycle.

I thought about it. Then it hit me like a bolt of lightning.

"I can't do it, Bucky."

"Come on. It'd be easy. No one's going to find out!"

"Look, my mom wouldn't do it, so I'm not doing it! I'm not a notary. There was a reason she wouldn't do it. It doesn't matter if no one ever found out. I'm not doing it."

Bucky got pissed and walked away.

I'd blown my chance to get in with the cool crowd. I was never going to be a motorcycle guy: I was going to be riding my ten-speed forever.

Then I heard a quiet voice behind me.

"You did the right thing."

I turned around. It was my mom. The window was open. She was standing in the shadows. She had heard the conversation.

"I just want you to know how proud I am that you did the right thing."

When you have your values, trust them, and make your decisions based on them, you'll be able to sleep at night. Remember, you're the one who has to get up and look at yourself in the morning. And if you're not comfortable with doing that based on a decision you've made, then you've made a bad decision, and you need to go back and fix it.

Your mom is always watching.

34

Chocolate, Chocolate, and More Chocolate!

With a plan, anything is possible.

I was driving home one afternoon, and I got a call from Colleen. Katelyn and Tim, our niece and nephew, wanted to have a sleepover at our house. They were five and six and a half years old. That is a little young to be wanting a sleepover, so I surmised that their mother, Kathy, was testing us to see what kind of babysitters we would be for future use.

I said yes. I can't say no to kids, but I didn't want to be anywhere near the babysitter list.

So what to do?

We needed a plan for the night. I wanted the kids to have the best time of their lives, but I also wanted their parents to say, "We're glad they had a great time, but we don't want you to babysit our kids anytime soon."

We didn't want to do anything wrong and we wanted the kids to have fun, but we also didn't want to become the designated babysitters. That's a tough tightrope to walk.

When it was time for the sleepover, I took off early from work. The kids came over, and I asked them what they wanted for dinner. They didn't know, so I suggested pizza, Kentucky Fried Chicken, or McDonald's. They wanted it all. Awesome!

Next, we went to the store to get snacks for the night.

We stopped at the candy aisle first, and I said, "Buy anything you want."

Their eyes got huge. "Really?"

Colleen started laughing because she was figuring it out.

The kids start putting bags of M&Ms and gummy bears and tons of chocolate in the cart. Next we headed for the cereal aisle with sugary cereals—Frosted Flakes and Cocoa Puffs. Then we went to the soda aisle and loaded up. Finally we headed for pizza, Kentucky Fried Chicken, and McDonald's on the way home.

After we unpacked their hoard back at the house, I asked, "What time do you usually go to bed?"

"We don't know. After the news, maybe?"

"What time do you want to go to bed?"

"We don't know. We've never been up after the news."

"Have you ever seen the sun come up?"

"No."

"Would you like to?"

"Yeah!"

"OK, that's what we will do tonight!"

So we built a massive fort with blankets and books all through the living and dining rooms. They had dinner and candy and soda. Colleen brought their favorite ice cream and some sundae making equipment home from her store, and we finished off dinner with ice cream sundaes.

We all settled down and watched TV.

Around 9:30, they started dozing off. I nudged them with my foot.

"Hey, wake up! The sun's not up yet!"

So we made hot chocolate and had more candy.

By eleven o'clock, they had chocolate on their faces and were sleeping soundly in front of the television. I was about to wake them up again, but Colleen stepped in. "Let them sleep."

I did, but I woke up at 5:00 a.m. and then woke them up.

"Hey, the sun's coming up. Let's go see it!"

They got up, excited and groggy. We watched the sun come up. I made pancakes with syrup.

"Have you ever had coffee?"

"No, can we?"

"Sure, just put a lot of milk and sugar in it."

Their mom was picking them up at 9:30. So I gave them all the candy and cereal and told them to put it in the bottom of their sleeping bags and hide it under their dirty clothes until they could get home and hide it in their rooms.

"How were they?" Kathy asked.

"They were terrific. Great kids."

Meanwhile they were dragging their sleeping bags down the stairs. With all the candy and cereal boxes stuffed in them, their sleeping bags looked like a snake that had just eaten a pig.

An hour later, we got the call from Kathy.

"What happened to my kids? They're cranky and tired."

She found the candy in the sleeping bags, and she wasn't happy.

Colleen said, "Hey Kathy, any time you want to send your kids over, we'd love to have them. They had such a great time!"

To this day, if you ask Katelyn or her brother about the best day of their lives growing up, they will say the sleepover.

And, for the record, we were never asked to babysit them overnight again.

Plan executed.

With a plan, anything is possible.

35

The Old Man of the Marsh

*Don't wait for the world
to solve your problems.*

On my mother's side, I had an Uncle Jack, and I didn't know Jack until later in my life (pun intended).

Eventually we became really close. One thing about Uncle Jack was that he noticed everything around him but rarely vocalized his complaints.

Jack bought a house in Revere, Massachusetts, in a section called Beachmont. As I've mentioned, his house was right on Belle Isle Marsh. It was on the water, and it was beautiful.

He built a deck so that you could see the marsh and the Boston skyline. On July 4, we could see all the fireworks in almost a 360-degree view.

Belle Isle Marsh originally flowed straight between Boston Harbor and the Atlantic Ocean. Over the years they blocked it off, cutting down the natural flow. It became a place where people would dump old tires and junk.

The tide also brought in trash, like old broken-away piers, styrofoam, and anything floating. There was no place for any of this stuff to go, so it would settle in the marsh. It was kind of a dump. One of the towns bordering the marsh had its dump right next to the marsh!

When Jack moved in, he'd take his rowboat out and row around the marsh. He noticed all this debris. He went into the local yacht club and talked to the people about the condition of the marsh. They all complained about it. He would listen. Everyone was waiting for someone else to do something about the problem.

The next day he spoke with the manager of the yacht club and asked, "How often do you have your dumpster emptied?"

The manager told him that the dumpster was picked up once a week and that it was rarely full. Jack told the manager he wanted to start cleaning up the marsh, getting rid of all the old tires, floating debris, and any trash. He asked the manager if he could put some of it in the yacht club's dumpster.

The manager thought Jack was nuts but said he could put three tires a week into the dumpster, along with any trash he collected, as long as he didn't fill the dumpster.

The next low tide, Jack headed out in the marsh. He rowed up to three tires, half buried in the muck. He cut a hole in the sides of each tire, ran a rope through them, attached huge chunks of styrofoam from the marsh to the tires, and left.

When the high tide came in, the styrofoam lifted the tires up. He rowed back to the floating tires, shook the muck from them, put each tire into his rowboat, rowed back to the yacht club, rolled the tires to the dumpster, and threw them in.

He did this for thirty years.

Twice a day we'd go out in the marsh, collect tires, and throw them away. (Weather permitting, of course.) He would stack the excess tires next to his shed so that he always had ones to throw into the dumpster, regardless of the weather.

It became Uncle Jack's mission to rid the marsh of these tires. He took out thousands of tires and tons of garbage. He would take the pieces of wrecked piers that floated in and cut them up for free firewood for his neighbors.

He became known as "The Old Man of the Marsh" because he cared about it and he loved it. Instead of complaining and waiting for somebody else to do something about it, he asked himself, "What can I do about this?"

I learned this lesson from him. We have a sidewalk in our neighborhood that goes through a long section between houses. It's two blocks from my house. There is a conservation area on the left and the road on the right. The road is 125 yards long. It was overgrown and awful to walk on. Neighbors complained about it, but it was somebody else's problem.

One day I put my tools in the back of my truck and drove to it. I started cleaning it. I started weed-whacking the overgrowth and cutting back the bushes. I got rid of all the things that were a problem. I mowed the tall grass, edged both sides of the side-walk, and got rid of all the cuttings and trash. The road became a nice place to walk.

I kept thinking about my Uncle Jack. This was my small way of giving back. I didn't clean up a marsh, but I did clean up 125 yards of sidewalk.

It felt good, and my neighbors really appreciated the small but significant impact on our neighborhood.

*Don't wait for the world
to solve your problems.*

36

Never Work Again

Know what you want before you start looking.

My nephew Greg and I have been close since he was two years old.

Shortly after he graduated college, I had him over for a celebration cigar. We were in my smoking room, having a nice Cuban cigar.

We talked about college and graduation. I asked him what kind of work he was going to do now that he had finished school.

He said that he'd had eight interviews so far. I asked him to tell me about them. He said that all of them went great and that he had five job offers.

"Wow! Tell me about the offers."

He described each in detail. There was quite a difference in salary: $50,000 a year at the low end and $90,000 at the high end.

"Which one are you going to take?"

In the back of my mind, I was thinking he should take the highest-paying one, because he had student loans to pay off.

Greg, sitting in a big leather chair, smoking the cigar, and blowing out the smoke, looked over and said, "I'm not taking any of them, Clark."

"You're not taking any of them? Why not?"

"Look. All my life, ever since I was a little kid, you've told me the same thing over and over: when you get a job you love, you will never go to work. I'm never going to love any of these jobs, so what's the point?"

I sat there, my jaw dropped. I started thinking, what else did I tell this kid that his parents are going to hate me for?

"Well, what do you want to do?" I asked.

He was always good with tools, so he said, "I'll find a job where I can learn trades. Welding, plumbing, carpentry—heck, I might even become an electrician. I'll find a job that will allow me to train and do all those things."

I was thinking, how are you going to do that? "Good luck, man" I said. "Keep me posted."

Six weeks later, Greg found a job as the maintenance director for a startup drug company. They had to manufacture new experimental drugs for a trial. He didn't know anything about the specialized equipment, but during the interview he said, "You know, my father set all this up for the previous company in this building. I bet if you talk to him, he'd be willing to come on board as a consultant to help me learn everything."

Sure enough, they did, and Greg got the job that he loved. That job led to another job and then to another. Right now he's in charge of all the maintenance for a town on Cape Cod, and he loves it.

Know what you want before you start looking.

37

Impressions, Impressions, Impressions . . .

Tell your own story.
Open your world to others.

I knew Larry when I was seventeen. He was twelve years older than me, married, with a son.

Larry knew how to tell a story! Before he started, he would look at the people in the room and choose the right story that would have immediate impact. He didn't tell the story just to tell the story. He told one that was on topic and right for everyone listening.

He never started with, "I'm going to tell you about . . ." He told me that was the kiss of death for any story. He started with where it happened and when it happened. This got everyone instantly engaged.

He kept it short. He knew we had short attention spans. He would go for five minutes. That was a long time. But often it was a lot shorter.

Larry also talked about the things that happened to him.

"It has to be your story. Don't take somebody else's story and try to make it yours. Because they'll figure it out. And when they figure out that it's not really you, you look like an asshole!"

So we need to tell our own story.

Finally, he thought in advance about the point. Why was he telling the story to this audience, and was it going to connect?

Larry was like a shaman sitting at a campfire. We were mesmerized by his stories. Most were funny, some not so funny, but each had a point. I listened and absorbed not only what he was saying, but how he was saying it.

I spent my teenage years from ages sixteen to twenty every Friday and Saturday night at Ron and Val's house, with Larry and Carol and other adult friends, listening to stories of their journeys to adulthood. They were only ten or twelve years older than me, but they were willing to share, and Larry's storytelling prowess made the nights fly by.

The ability to tell your story is critical. In fact, if you don't know how to tell your story in a compelling way, somebody else will tell it for you. And quite often less compellingly and probably not to your benefit.

However the willingness to share your story can have even more impact on the people around you.

We all have unique knowledge, insight, and perspective that can shine light on unknown paths for others. I am forever grateful that I was included in Larry's storytelling and to be the youngest member of those who got to hang out at Ron and Val's during those years.

Tell your own story.
Open your world to others.

About the Author

Clark Merrill travels the world, training trainers to deliver Dale Carnegie's courses. He is one of only thirty-seven Carnegie Masters who train and certify new Dale Carnegie trainers worldwide. He has been working with trainers and developing client relationships for the last thirty-one years. He is also an executive coach and motivational speaker.

Clark's prior experience includes multi-store and warehouse operations for Hickory Farms of Ohio in South Florida, with five year-round retail locations, two seasonal retail locations, and a seasonal production warehouse.

Clark worked his way up from busboy to general manager of Black Caesar's Forge, an historic 200-seat steakhouse in South Florida.

Clark's also served as director of food and beverage for Bay State Cruise Company in Boston. Bay State operated six vessels on Boston Harbor, ranging in size from 50 to 1,100 passengers. Bay State was the number two beer retailer in Boston during the summer months, after Fenway Park.

Clark was district manager and director of franchising for Brigham's Ice Cream Restaurants in New England. Brigham's restaurants included eighty-seven stores and an ice cream manufacturing plant in Arlington, Massachusetts. He was instrumental in developing Brigham's franchise operating systems.

As you can see, Clark likes people and food!

Clark is a widower. His wife, Colleen, passed away in January 2018. She was his best friend, mentor, and relentless coach. She was also "fairy godmother" to their niece Katelyn and an awesome aunt to all the other nieces and nephews.

Colleen is the inspiration for this book. She is missed every second of every day by Clark and anyone that knew her.

CPSIA information can be obtained
at www.ICGtesting.com
Printed in the USA
JSHW050034090922
30204JS00002B/2